Poems of meaning and symbolism

Poems of meaning

and

Symbolism

Jeffrey B. Holl

Produced in affiliation with the Freedom of Expression component of the Canadian *Charter of Rights and Freedoms*, **Canadian Heritage** directive (see *fundamental freedoms* section (2b)).

First Edition
Created, Edited and Typeset in Canada

I.C.H. Publishing, Wpg., MB.

Library and Archives Canada

ISBN: 978-1-7752848-9-5

Cover image © Shutterstock

For one that is before all else, yet ever-transcending . . .

CONTENTS

A Resonating Glimpse

Twilight here beyond these walls, of dreams where glimmered
Memories,
And where the universe convened
A light reveals an inner self—

What are we but this that's shone
A trillion years of finite time?

There shimmering the portals' climb
From skies to truth
This life is reaching
Forward pathways through the dust,

Where we descend from Earth as souls
That hold from birth undying sight,
To search the edge from there outside
Transcending this the moment sees,

Beckoning the visions where we ponder
What the spirit frees,

From there toward our folding minds
We fused our Being from where it seemed
Projected ever to the truth,
Unreal while whole
Yet there conceived—

More radiant than what were freed
A resonating glimpse.

With Nothing There in Sight

Be it through the pathways our existence foraged,
Forward histories we became,
There's something onward to the dream
For what's revealed emboldens time—
We are escapes from where we'd bred
And purposed means of symbols' claim;
Yet this that heeds the passageways
Toward what's this that holds our minds.

Nowhere thoughts imagined,
Or the enterprise of sordid hopes,
The shields of what these escapades
Might will the notions we amend—
For greater than the lives of thieves
We'll bring the real ones to an end;
And float our own salvation where
We've come to rend what no lives saved.

For where we do perceive within
The world is more than what it seems,
It is what's closed to those that gave
And freed to those that it defends—
Where we conceive, we realize
The spectre of a shadowed beam
That fights for what invokes the light
With less than what we'd visualize.

And there no domination's bout
Embattled would project the skies,
For atmospheres receive our vision
More than fields that hold the night—
Wherein we seed what's thrown from souls
Descending ever as we rise;
Beginnings are the face of those
That see with nothing there in sight.

As a Virulence

The firmaments transforming life's enduring
Genesis transcending,
We become composed of matter
Spirits see within the mending,
Healing spaces where we're forming
Symbolized from where we're thrown—
And held within the armaments
That glimpsed beyond what we had known.

Through eyes of wonder watching what is there
And leaves the stratosphere,
We're borne upon the ground and shattered
That we've blown toward the edge,
Where we may wander nothing matters
But what's become of fear—
Where we've undone the ever after
To the places we were led.

From violence adorning rife enduring
Menaces ascending,
Overcoming foes that gathered
Bodies freed from our appearing,
Stealing faces radiating
Canonized as though they're owned—
Wielded as a virulence
To starve what it had grown.

Wilderness That We'd Undone

Toward a wandering, an edge of time,
Thoughts transcending through a mind,
The spaces that we'd occupied are
Shadowed where we're meant to hide—
Unfolding memories surpassed
A clearing of the woods becomes
A new beginning where our fates
Arise before what days had cast.

The whispers of the soul are one,
And we arrive to free the skies
From wilderness that we'd undone
To flesh we seed where we'd survived—
For years the spirits fed the night,
And meaning cast this world beyond;
Through setting suns that held our pride
To dancing mirrors before our eyes.

Closing doors with open hearts
And seizing symbols from within,
There is a truth that shows the scars
And places where we shan't return,
To lights that shine where we'd begin
To see what's here remaining still,
What slips the sight from where it burned
From trees to soil and Earth to stars.

Become

Through solace we abandoned minds that held the world
beyond
    A reason that the foiled consumed,
    Of opened arms where we'd subsumed
    The nights escaped and days forlorn—

More than we condemned to be
Of beings beyond a world of forms,
We're thrown outside an endlessness
Of life's presumed bewildered state,
Where what we are has soared to traipse
The meaning that our hearts must seek,
The sun is mirrored where we speak
Of moments that depart the gaze,
To rise outside where we were phased
Of chosen spirits floating there,

The truth is where a light projects
Of signified and abstract dreams,
We hide inside where we convened
Upbraiding what our souls declared,
Where we preside yet faltered through
Travails of this a mind still sees,

Horizons where we've found the freed
Despaired that we had never been,
More than what's for skies to seed
But this that leaves behind its signs,
Forever from an Earth where time
Becomes where this forbids our fate,

Discovered where we stood to wait
For what had somehow been displaced,

We'll be the search toward a chase
That breathes a presence through this world,
Where this is less than what we'd fused
But more than what had been escaped,
Throughout the energies of space
And where the memories we'd face
Become.

Where We Must Accede

Beneath these arms, we stand as those delivered
Bodies to a soul,
Becoming this that's freed
And this that's lain,
We shimmer through a folding limber
Form from where existence reigned—

The purpose of our Being had failed
Should we be less that this that seeds
The reason we'd renounced our deeds,
To falter through an ambush
Where the forthright sounds of life
Forever scorned where we recede,

As this throughout the fetters
Where the breath we uttered
Pushes life,
Beyond a netherworld of matter
Symbolled where we must accede—

These dreams confound the night
As this which flatters every dying deed;
But we've projected through our toils
To wither from the space we'd freed—

Shattered wills depart where torn
These foiled and growing doubts appeased;
Threads we'd borne from escapades
As weathered, mourned, admonished days
Return the sun from where the sight
Conceived what nature had released—

The future is displaced of nowhere
We were formed and not betrayed.

Beheld

Where the vision tells the sight that there is no beginning,
Horizons find the edge of this
That leads somewhere we've yet to seek,
Where from this meaning we'd undone
Much more than just an ending—
Teetering within the night,
Thrown from our mortality
To reason what's beyond a place
Where what we are is mending.

Crushed, consumed and radiant light
We seize each breath unbound by time,
The legions of the portals chimed
What's given its resounding—
The world is energy of mind
And we of concepts souls astound,
From where we'd reach there are no signs
That furthers spirits through the ground.

Of hearts too blind where we persist
And beings withering no more,
The tempests of what's left behind
Reside where there's nothing before—
What we perceive, we hold as this
Disguised by something through our selves
Yet hide with ease what we have seen
To cast aside what we'd beheld.

Where Those Emboldened Flowed

The sun sleeps, embers of the night are fleeting
    Daylights mourned and warned evinced—
    A glowing of the dark inside …

    Seen beyond the torch and glimmer
    Shadows echo where we'd pierced;
    Heavens through a cold that's whimpered
    Meaning torn beyond a glimpse,

    Becoming this that's sees in winter
    Undulating as the stars;
    As those that ever flee distemper
    Finding twilight through those eyes …

    From orbs of temples glowing meaning
    Time is resonating as the folds
    Of this that's never waiting,
    Soaring, seeking, moments died—

    Lives escaped from torment's splintered
    Borne from this that holds me in;
    Beauty that were scorned cascading
    Ever through what truth's belied.

    Forever thrusts of minds are these
    Of semblances where fire is fading,
    Upwards where the spirits rose—

    Hiding's where we're never far
    From days where those emboldened flowed.

Transcending what is ever waiting
And the ruse is left behind—
The night's of making this that darts
Toward those skies where we were clothed.

Breed

Touched the revolutions as a radiance beyond the sight,
Cutting Earth's abandonment,
Perceived there's nothing left of time—
Shined beyond the planet
With a light that seeds and freed the skies!
Heavens bleed the stars condemned
And souls become a world of minds.

Trudged throughout the passageways
Where we depart never to die,
Rushing from what's shadowed
There is more than what we had denied—
Barriers pushed what followed,
Universes where no torment reigns;
Folding holes of fortresses
That fought beyond a world of pain.

Ruptured hearts of emptied whims
And ravaged flesh torched to the bone,
Damaged presences begin
To prod the blood for weeping stones—
Sorcery where truth remained
Redeeming scavengers decreed;
Streets all littered by the skin
Too bold and aged to hold their breed.

What the Moonlight Cried

Toward an open door we see symbolically, and pierce its
haze,
    Inside there is a world of what we were
    Before a hastening...

    We, the shadows of the past are
    Captured never by our ways—
    But looking where the darkness ends
    To where our souls are wandering,

    To search for this that frees its hold
    Upon the meaning we'd conveyed,
    The eyes perceive what lives behind
    While reasoning beyond what we might
    Posit from within our core,

    Treading where the windows seized
    Of this revealed that we'd betrayed,
    The stars have tears for this that needs
    Illumining a closing space,
    Where monads' signified embrace
    Beleaguered what the moonlight cried,

    The wounds repaired what's been denied
    And life is hidden where it's strange,
    Somewhere where one belief had changed
    The truth from where it's never died
    But lives where it were raised.

Clear

Where space defines the distance, and distance is time,
Echoed memories falling.

Displaced, yet crumbling—

Where shades of opened universes
Float the trees and hold the mind;

This wide ensnared and portal chased
Convened.

Screamed, the dark idolatries,
Marbled shapes of stone erased—

Held in hand a world for those
That formed what wisdom's never faced;

Life is questioning . . .

Undulating mourning waste
And folding torn berated worth;

From ashes borne into the sound
Of no one's listening.

Silence. . .

The obfuscating haste through which
We ponder something infinite,

And finitude is nothing
But the edge from where we've leapt the ground—

Here.

Out toward the meaning,
Where the skies consumed what spirits found
To clear.

Poems of Engagement or Denial

Unwed Within Ourselves

It dawns on those for whom the world is finite that we'd each
Relinquish what's within,
More than shadowed nothing
That we're bound and tied
To grieve what wisdom's inner sight
Conceived and wedged,
Between what we'd believed
And where the fallows of this truth were lain—

We're seconds from where we begin
But just the same, maligned to gain
The things we'd thought were to exist
For this, the meaning of an age
That we resisted time itself,
Determinate of lives confessed
Assuaged where we were lingering,
As towers bred a courage higher
Cowards held upon their chest,
We're are enslaved to where this Earth
Revealed the chains of endlessness,

Graves are emptied harnesses
Bereaved where we had not addressed
The blackness where it won't appear,
We'll spend another thousand years
Renouncing days within arrest,
Where we were swayed and there betrayed
And despots rule as scavengers,
Alive to free the tyrants from those
Ways by which the savages
Become the ones for whom we've raised
A life unwed within ourselves.

Days Where History's Lingering

Of this which has no form, yet it is Being, an essence more
Than what is here within transcendence—

Exposed from darkness,
Shattered light ...

Illumined—thrown form nature
Into seeing far beyond this life;

The Other from an Earth perceived
From shadows beckoning the truth.

More than we might understand,
Burning ashes held a world
Of souls compelled by innocence,

Feel beyond every command,
The sun sits on its perch;
Creatures born are bound to yield,
A presence where they may be none;
There is more than lasting worth where
Kissing wounds we're bound to heal—

Some escape what is conceived
Toward the moments we'd become
Less than what had pierced the wind;

Of souls that fought the pacts we'd sealed
Undone that they had been received—
Folding through the passageways
Of radiant beams to glowing nights,

The sun is setting where the fields
Revealed the stars are flickering ...

Outside is a place within
Where mirrors sparkled spirits' minds,
Though corridors we'd wield betrayed
The days where history's lingering.

Unforbidden Trace

There is the broken opened world,
　And closing edges through the space,
And endlessness that holds the time
　Toward a meaning rendered there—
The symbols weeping and their signs,
　The grip that slips where intertwined,
And this that folds within the mind
　Inside the memories we'd faced.

Alive to see what would begin,
　Yet to forbid is to escape,
What had been given is the path
　Of this the road we'd chose to find—
And of the one that one might take
　The answer lies where life remains
From places we'd return again
　Should this be what had been behind.

For those that lay within the dust
　Where shadows cast enlightened shrouds,
The days become of this that sees
　Where visions cast a being thus—
To never seize what failed to end
　Or live beyond transcending souls
The spirits leave what crumbled us
　From this that's held within these moulds.

That what is here resounds the skies
　Yet stands here filled from soil to dust,
Where grounds are waiting for the bold
　To glimpse outside of those repairs—

And eased of darkness from the eyes
  We'll find somewhere within this sight
An unforbidden trace of air
  That folds from spaces we'd recoiled.

Fastening

The light of you, where darkness fades to black;
Shadowed frozen stars become,
This world is ever crumbling,
Radiating boundless souls—

Folding dreams consume the space
That throws from what emboldens time,
What appears is less than whole
But lives beyond what's beckoning.

Where shattered heavens do descend
Illumined spirits reach the night,
As we are those that seek to heal
What gone from what we'd once defined.

Toward despairs that search delight
There is no less than what we feel
But this residing where our sight's
An obfuscation's glimmering ...

We cry uncovered and exposed
From this that hides away the truth,
Therewith to spoil what had deposed
A meaning that had been revealed—

Ascending from the earth to sky,
Freed of minds embattled there,
We preach what no one real could know
And topple what we're fastening.

Fathoming

Stages of the monad peering, there beyond our immanence,
Outside the inner space
We'd hide ourselves,
And storm cascading
Passages—

Spirits chimed the echoes
At the thresholds of a wandering,
No anguished thrust of torment sees
But leads a pathway we'd deceived—
Amidst illumined, flickering...

Shedding dusts of time that pledged
Abstractions leaving trust denounced;

There is a wall from where we're bound
Unwed with where we're gathering—

Broken steps toward the mount,
Of undulating souls become;

As where the beacon does resound,
There is a meaning and its wounds—

Scars reclaim what worlds confound
And left nowhere their fathoming.

Trammel Where We Hide

Thrust from Earth to form
Escaped into the night,
The minds carried the storms,
The storms carried the light—
And there where we appeared
The wreckage fought the skies:
A spectre of our ghosts
Became what we had feared.

Borne from stone and ash,
Chained to our beliefs
The truth is nowhere passed
The place where we still grieve—
Cascading spirits climb
For sparkling moulds to clash:
There is what won't remain
Where freedom's will conceived.

From shadowed blackened suns
Illumined we become,
To seize what were confined
And die somewhere inside—
To live with what we'd done
But trammel where we hide,
The pathways smeared the signs
Emancipating pain.

Trust from birth to norm,
Berating us in sight,
The blind carried the warned,
The warned carried the might—

And where the broken leered
The carnage had been torn,
From there where anger boasts
That it had bled the tears.

Charms engulfed in flames,
Joy condemned to death,
Fractured pleasure's blame
Where it had been too real—
Redeemed where nothing's left
Through endless doubts maligned,
Banished from the theft
The dead were bound to feel.

From windowed worlds where run
The meaning from the heart,
To where emotions flow
Throughout the woes they weave—
Enlightened moments bend
What ends where nothing' gone:
Horizons we'd defend
Belong where we would leave.

Glimpsing

Where universal or contingent, we are objects to a space
That cease to rise inside our wisdom,
Acceding what is there conceived
And where the lasting of our fusion's
More than what the eyes would hold ...

We are those that must perceive
The skies where tread the barriers,
We're prized to heed what's gone untold
Unhinged this world its carriers,
To hide nowhere but where the sun
Must set ablaze the souls that seek—

We've become what nothing rends
But cries that live where none should speak
Projecting endlessly beyond ...

Plateaus we rendered from the edge
Where Bacchus soaked the night with bread
And lined the waste with what we'd weave
To leave behind where it had longed—

A place the planet found misled,
From passageways within the swell
And fields where truth were of the dead,
Piercing images where dwelled
The torpid glimpses of a life
Of mind.

The Signs of Our Birth

In the beginning, there were those that came and sought,
   What were steeped in a darkness if only for taking,
   And this that were never too far away ...

And the earth in an image of spirits forbidding,
That the signs of our birth
Never led to decay.

There where the sun always sets in the distance,
The heavens are less
That what history brought;

Though what it is not, is only for making
The miseries cry
With what lies there betrayed.

And what wields the becoming of our veneration,
For the trails and the promises,
Sold where they're bought.

Yet still we know it is never sleeping,
Yet the stars all have time
For where dreams go astray.

 As the fortunes of man,
And the touch of the night
Slip to the place where the wise are not silenced,
Shadows of the clouds had once told of the air
Becoming of where this is tabled in mind—

And the blossoming skies that unfold into kindness
Resemble the moments as shields to the soul,
Never crumbling where violence had led to those sights
Where the memories held were once thoughts never blind.

Of an ending we know not what's there for this world,
Only these emptied and striving repairs—
Ours is the meaning with our heads to a wall;
That the other side still stands there behind,
And not for the worries great or absurd
But the stories we'd told
That true hearts will declare.

Harrowing Obtrusion

Into itself, an existential notion inward
Yet here unconfined,

There is nowhere the harried climbs
Of stasis flooded boundless skies—

Barricades assuaged and fallows' signs
Where atmospheres absconded night,

And lore of this that founds all time
As bending shadows crawled the space,

A harrowing obtrusion
There beyond no world's replies.

Rends envisaged borne in haste
The hallows chimed what billowed through
The bended moments torn away,

To cry the wistful chides into
A dying of the portal phased,

Assuaged and contemplated guise
Belies the maze and ploughs us through
These sights that mend the human race,

From eyes perceiving this we'd faced
Outside the souls that pierced the ruse
Into believing more than lies.

The Seer

The seer shines the lamplight cross, where soared and dreamed
    A wandering edge,
The escapades to free the space
    Of wisdom from where moments slip
From passages nothing condemns,

We're bound and heaved from soil to ledge
A meaning of unspoken means—

The wonder cries "Amend what's seized!"
    To hide the dominations' plot;
The seething memories of ought
    Deride inside the reasoned skies ...

Into the opened eyes we've heaved
    From Earth to time where minds conflate,
This soul is energy of world
    And we an everlasting fate
That's risen from what limits rend,

Projected where spirits descend
    To hide no radiance of Being,
Where we portend to be of meaning
    More than what's despaired the world—

We've found the crawling paths inured
    For nothing blurred within the dark
Beyond.

The Prize

More than what the mind could hold,
Less than what it there might need,
Bound toward the edges' bold
That night had offered no escape—

Higher than ionospheres
And grounded where the memories chimed,
Thrown from bodies' fragile mould
To where these dreams are escapades.

Consciousness that leads somewhere,
Beyond the Earth but where the skies
Become each moment we'd behold
A glimpse inward that captures time—

Through the light we'd symbolized
And wayward past the days of old,
There is no wisdom we might find
That reasons gold into the wise.

And there the streams of dusted fields
Conceived these means to shield the souls
From where this ends in plenitude
Resisting surged, revealed the prize!

inside

Perceived something inside that now has gone
    a darkness fell upon my world,
That ever I could be so blind
    There's something left that I still need—
Yours is to remember what were for the light
    And this that's dwelling nowhere found,
Upon the places where we'd find
    A life that heals reality.

The universe departs the spaces—
    those that lost returned to shine,
For better there is this unbound
    where time becomes of memories,
It is for us to know the signs
    and what's been thrown from spirits' wills—
As for power, there is only as one is
    toward those thoughts that have been seized.

Something Invisible

Spending moments lost in thought
 Without reasons for thinking—
That what is, is and what is not
Becomes of something clear;
We might mend the distance we're immersed
With more than only sinking
As we're floating somewhere on the Earth
And never really here.

For presence also is an absence
Pondering things outside the real,
We hold ideas within ourselves
And find what's never really there—
What we are to one another
Necessarily is concealed
As what is found only discovered
Drifting far beyond our stare.

For instance, take a thing disclosed,
Burrowed through the depths of time—
Plunging from the highest heights
Where there's no way to capture it;
And what is there becomes opposed
Within a mould we'd fracture if
We'd get a glimpse of what there is
Escaping there before our minds.

This space is as an empty world—
Filled with less than what it is,
Totality is nothing
And infinity impossible—
Things depart where they begin
And keep existing where there not;
That what the human race has got
Becomes something invisible.

Ionospheres

We bridged the space transcending waters thrown
From gulfs beyond the gaze,

Mirrored the void
From whispers, faint despoiled escapes
And wandering...

Fading atmospheres of sight
The darkness spilled into the stars,
Heeding vanity's contempt
That's wed to this that painted suns—

Of skies the wombs led blood from light
And felt the condemnations leave,
The confluence of our dominion
Shattered as the world becomes.

And we depart beginnings
With what time portrayed never to weave,
A flourishing beyond the night
That sees more than we'd overcome—

Sheds the moon's repairs into the flowing
Radiance of Being,

Pondered through the stratosphere
Of this that hastened thoughts outrun—

Reason that these minds condoned
The very things that we've redeemed,
Revealed of souls that sensed within
What lives to seize ionospheres.

Restored

Borne of spirits shining searchlight
Into forms we bond the stars,
Fixtures thrust the skies we'd freed
Beyond where disappeared the doors,
Lured were emptied moulds of space
That shattered time within perceived,
Obscured as minds believing
Where we swore that none were there believed...

Moments of the souls inviting
Everlasting thoughts we'd traced,
Becoming this that pierced the wombs
Outside where lives are hinging deeds—
Of nights' retreat where none have bloomed
The village sleeps the symbols' dreams,
As this which feeds what's been erased
Contemptuous the frenzied moons.

Alive we seed enlightened holes
That seize abstraction from its means,
To rise from sight appeased in ferment
Blithe the eyes conceived consumed,
Of images that we've abandoned
There where crumbling curtains teased
A being within the nature
That restored a beauty we'd resumed.

Mazes

Never to a dying soul becomes an age of endlessness,
We breathe the wreckage of our days
And rise from where the darkness shunned
These ambushed moments of a rage
That scales the walls that built us in,

We're somehow there condemned to sway
Where mortal through an aimlessness
That fled the wounds we'd freed of sin,
Where worlds repealed the tracts of worth
That foiled the passions of the gaze,

To heed what's where we'd cry the sun
    And banish what's beyond the haze,
Into an atmosphere of this
    That postures threads of doubts bereaved,

We'd topple this that were believed
    Abstracting what's upon the Earth,
To seize the time with living more
    Than passing from inception's birth
That died inside more than the stars
Through floating edges of the night,

    Toward the passageways where flown
Were savage shadows of the light,

    From ashes' dust and love concealed
Our memories depart the mind,
If only to abandon this
That led from stables there revealed,

From where what's tabled of the blind
To mazes where a second guess
Assailed the natures we'd redeemed,
The fabled hours spirits convened
To push beyond the pacts we'd sealed,

Harnessing the symbols that this
World had broken from our hearts,
And bled the skies toward what's gone
And leads outside where dreams depart
And minds begin to heal.

Perceiving

To see a distance within, to hold the time as though
We fall before illumined minds, and hide behind
Our reasons to begin—

To rise inside where we reside
And capture where we've been.

Perceiving this beyond ...

To seize the moment where we'd die before
We'd freed ourselves again.

We are the seekers of time—

For what we'd sought were there before
The heights we had to climb.

To seed existence from within, and fold our lives to throw
A rise before we shine as opened wide
Through closures of the din—

Descending where this life's alive
For longing as we've dreamed.

To liberate our souls from where
Our liberties had beamed.

Conceiving this beyond ...

To free the torment from its lore
Where memories eased the pain.

We are the vespers of minds—

For what we had believed were there
Through obfuscating signs.

To seek our reason from within, to mould
Our fates before the time, escaping there outside
The thoughts that dwell nowhere herein.

No Other Meaning

Abounding regions' pledge of night,
From there inside a pondering ...
No wisdom's leaving folds beyond
This reason's light, our wandering—

Through edges of transcending storms
We're bold outside corporeal form,
And held within where souls behold
There is no Other meaning—

Fleeting sights become this mould,
Through one that flows from blood to stone,
Where we depart what heals the world
To shed untold an Earth in time—

Waged from spirits' slumbered tones
No shattered bones believe the dark,
Yet we perceive more than we'll own
And into shadows seize our minds.

The future heeds the blessed where signs
Conceive the moments we assuaged,
The last conviction of our lives
Becomes what's real within our age.

And torments grieve the lasting sieve
Illumined and redeemed exposed,
Revealed are forms where visions leave
Within this hedged upon the skies.

Toward what beckons what's bestowed
Upon the weeping, sprouting leaves,
What flows from here inside is bold
And nowhere turns to silent cries.

Our Minds Engaged

Behind blockades of world and mind,
Appearance shattered this beheld
Of life's bewildered throws of souls,
We're not condemned to reason
But resist the spaces we behold,
And float as those unbound by time
To see the passage that we'd heal,
That where our place were not confessed
It heeds what's there, a beacon
At the edge of Earth and our decline,

The hold upon the bind reveals
The burgeoning where we'd convened,
Assuaged of this that posits dreams
But sees the real beyond all doubt,
That we determined what were sought
And foraged through the pathways there,
We're blind within what we declare
Toward an inward glimpse that holds,

Without a closing door we'd fought
To freedom's ending we're confined,
But through what's told we've intertwined
As life's never bewildered ought,
We'd feed this rise upon the lands
And hide what history had forgot,
To seize the skies with what we'd wrought,

Reprised the ambush of our days,
That we would free this landscape from
The thoughts that never would betray,
Should we receive or leave astray
What being hereto must understand,

The night's escape within command
And what the thresholds had believed,
That we would never have conceived
Of something more than this we'd bought,

As lives undone we had begot
A meaning less than this we'd known,
Upon those movements we'd condoned
Of this that led where limits rend
The inner truth where we'd ascend
As those unbound throughout the age—

And never will this world dissuade
The cries projected there outside,
The inner realm where we reside
And this will be where we commence,
There is what's here beyond defense
Forever and alas, the end
Of this that limits what's inside
And brings us to where we'd amend
What's real our minds engaged.

Poems of Certainty and regret

Nothing of the Storm

Reflections mirrored within a soul
    The night embraced in emptiness,
The shadows of the world still hold
    A message that's been set adrift—

    We are nothing of the storm,
Blessed of peace and time to breathe;
    Of fallowed, furling temperament
Where eyes are bold upon the seas ...

Swooning ties that bind the skies
    To hide behind what's been appeased,
The shelters of the womb undressed
    A rise where spirits' light consumed—

    Obfuscating shades of mind
Bewilder hapless hearts naïve,
    As we conceived where boldness flows
The memories where Earth still blooms.

The moon is savage—Wisdom's tears
    Of conscious lies where truth appeared,
Torrential years where no world cried
    Believing those that fought our doom—

Proffered through no opened arms
This future's sold for humankind;
  But through these ruins where fates unwind
What's ours still there exists inside.

Thrown outside the water's edge,
  Of fortune's visage unassuaged—
A moment forms this borne of signs
  To flood what meaning's had to hide;

  Into this wedge within our age
Becoming what is real presides
  The convocation where we tread
To see beyond the scope of mind.

Of Nights Relinquished to the Seeds

A light salvation's symbolized, becoming through an
emptied space,
    The one where we are objects
    Of the obfuscating moments
    That we fold from time to free our souls,
    We are in contemplation's hold
    And seeing what is to perceive,
    Of nights relinquished to the seeds
    That plant a signified within,
    Where are we that we won't begin
    To reason more than is an art?

    Of willingness and wisdom's heart
    With what is held within the world,
    Where revelation's ever heard
    We seek a passage through the dark,
    That what is there unveils the throws
    Of those that healed upon the reefs—
    The shores where crashed our last reprieve
    That we were ever to this land
    The spirits beckoning.

Where No Memories We'd Faced Obscured

Through solace we abandoned minds that held the world
beyond
  A reason that the foiled consumed,
  Of opened arms where we'd subsumed
  The nights escaped and days forlorn—

  More than we condemned to be
  Of beings beyond a world of forms,
  We're thrown outside an endlessness
  Of life's presumed bewildered state,
  Where what we are has soared to traipse
  The meaning that our hearts must seek,
  The sun is mirrored where we speak
  Of moments that depart each gaze,
  To rise outside where we were phased
  Of chosen spirits floating there,

  The truth is where a light projects
  Of signified and abstract dreams,
  We'll hide inside where we convened
  Upbraiding what our souls declared,
  Where we preside yet faltered through
  Travails of what a mind still sees,

Horizons where we've found the freed
Despaired that we had never been,
More than what's for skies to seed
But this that leaves behind its signs,
Forever from an Earth where time
Becomes of what forbids our fate,

Discovered where we stood to wait
For what had somehow been displaced,
We'll be the search toward a chase
That breathes a presence through this world,
Where this is less than what we'd fused
But more than what had been escaped,
Throughout the energies of space
And where no memories we'd faced
Obscured.

A League of Cult

The edges of the outside where the hidden spirits bind,
Identities become undone,
Tarnished epigrams perplexed
Redemption's vision's blind—

Existences exalting fault,
Vanishing unsung;
The dead consuming what were flung
From stages never shown through time …

Illuminating life craft,
Perspicuous tumult,
Punishing from forces
Punching beauty to assault—

Cunning epitaphs and cinched,
The wisdom's thrust condemned,
There are no Others than the ones
That formed a league of cult.

Powers driven madness,
Watching minds pretend,
The mirror senses something
Inside a fear beyond—

Crushed attempts were banished,
Futile memories swayed;
Where lives were not yet finished
Reality still bends.

Crunching mental towers
Fondled magic cheers,
A moment stitched the fabric
Of bodies that were wronged.

Plumes of trust betrayals waged,
Of vanities that fled;
Damaged portals opened leers
As torments plundered for the caged—

Ours were never to be led,
What's pledged the bred from truth's disguise—
There where statues spent the years
And flowers fed upon the haze.

Wooden Chains

Of blood drenched rains or ocean's stars ... souls
condemned
    Or wed to hearts —

These wooden chains won't hold me in;

Life escapes into the wind ...

The scars of souls have fed the light —
There is what's happening inside;

Where is the moment we ignite
To never find where to begin?

Of depths we feigned and potions ours, moulds that tend
To spirit guards —
These golden plains won't hold me in;

Life escapes into the wind ...

The bards of time are blessed the night,
And this will be where we might hide;

There is no torment to invite
Where there is something left to win.

Afterword

Ever be the light of truth, this that echoed through the darkness of the dreams inhabiting existence where were lain the fortressed mind where thou had been sworn—never to ravage from the compass of our being the spaces where we dwell as purities undamaged by the forsaken wills of the spirits undone by history's savage claims. The tides are turning less than the winds that blow into the world as it settles in the dust of the explorations that have governed the meaning of this age; and we will to hoist a domain of emptiness to its place in the finitude of humankind's reclamation of the natures that bind us to the soul of the Earth's core. Never more but to see with vision more than the transcendental excursions of the projections seated within the eyes might ever propose to perceive, as the sun sets upon a planet of despair and of woe. We are the seeds of hope that curse the wretched and hold to account a reality that forbids beauty and the magnitudes of radiance that heighten the evocation of what propels our ideals beyond the limitations of the domination of what represents the totality of this moment into a universe of possibility and the powers of creativity and resolve. The mind is an instrument of its ownership over the ambitions governing intellectual pursuit and held within the spirit as a force unto itself—the will of humanity pervades each interstice where aspirations are only quelled by the oppression of the truth and the gravity of the objects that hold us upon the soil; as beings resigned to an absence of trust and a residence in the heavens of our own regret and universal compromise. The future lies in what is held to be the past of a purpose that may be sensed before it is realized, and the senses of our kind have dimmed to the propositions of a culture that ceases to excise its representation of an attainment of universality as a space where the gathering of the monuments to posit existence as sustainable to its own purposiveness is less than the natural impetus elevating the core experiences of the human race as a generative appropriation of the true form of what drives humankind into the elements of its most vital unyielding and transformative capacitation—we are likely to become extinct as a result of our own attempt to supply the economy within the desperational furtherance of the fervour galvanizing the confluence of symbols that reign positing realisms undulating within the memories of a lost and forgotten amalgam of the dispossessed.

Restorative Justice

To you and only you, this fate resides in the hands of the many, yet is condemned to the notions of one.

Where we are is where there is nothing, yet where something there exists.

Mind is soul more than money, more value than the worth of what is external to human contemplation.

Memory is the value of meaning ... where there is no meaning there is no value and only memory of what should not possess existence.

Hope is the transformation of meaning into value, and the signification of what has been valued by the meaning of hope as valuation in-itself.

There is purpose to things that have no use if the will to possess them is less than the desire to use them without the possession of what worth these objects have yet to attain.

Life is a pursuit that is pleasurable where its fruits have been borne by the lives that are more fruitful than the pleasures that have been borne by them.

In order to possess reality, one must first possess the deceptions from which it had originated as reason's singular purpose and aim—the truth is never persuaded by what had driven it from its moment of falsity; yet always by those very means conveyed.

The desire to pursue with contemptuous envy the objects that are thought to determine a meaning for this existence is ever fleeting, and knowledge comes only to those that apprehend reality as it is determined by the sense through which the truth may be expressed as an end by which the means is never within justification, yet always within the conception of what had driven reality as an exposition of the authenticity of the content through which its form is to be realized.

Life has no obstacles that have not become exposed through the attempt to fulfill what is beyond the comprehensibility of those that would otherwise wish to reproduce the means of existence through what is understood rather than what is told.

Being is rendered through the experience of reality as a purpose unto itself—designed as a world that has reached awareness of the very existence that has been furnished by the natural properties in existence therewith.

The appearance of wisdom is a representation that brings with it the presupposition that images to the mind may be perceived through the conjuring of what is purposive to the conception of what is derived as a symbolization of what condones the real as a truth for those that seek it in earnest.

The natural progress of humanity is a space where meaning is resolute and being is a content that is both substance and appearance—its reality exists within a meaning purposive to the means through which it is to transcend to the boundaries of its own fecundity and contingent identical articulation.

The spaces where a mind is delivered from its own illusions are the same as where a conscience reveals the purity of conception as a reality that is beyond the deceptive powers of an involuntary imagination.

Reason's articulation of the purposes that are revealed by the effects generated by causal conceptions are mere accidents, delivered by a false sense of judgment, rendered by the passions of an undisciplined mind.

The purpose of humanity is to fulfill the meaning that is incarnate to the nature through which thoughts are identical to themselves in kind, and different to the musings of an otherness to which reality has become opposed.

The processes through which one identifies the principles governing the purposes of humanity are never in conflict with the correct interpretation of reality, as it is seated in the mind as universally concrete and only particular to the judgments of one for whom the truth is irrevocable beyond the shadow of a doubt never to be cast aside.

www.ingramcontent.com/pod-product-compliance
Lightning Source LLC
Chambersburg PA
CBHW031901170626
46807CB00004B/1845